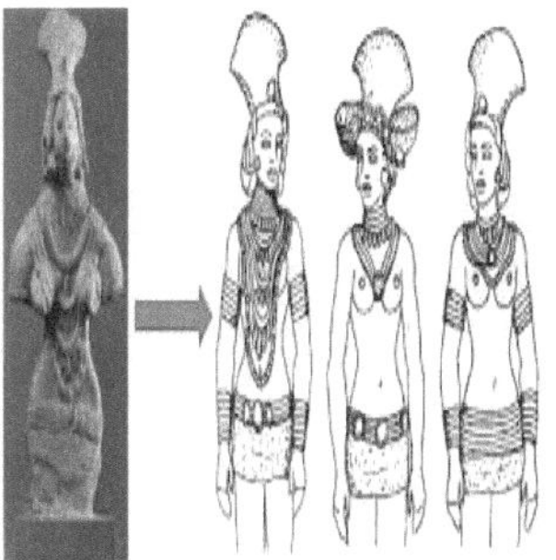

Old EGYPT:

- Old Egyptian garments allude to apparel worn in old Egypt from the finish of the Neolithic time frame (before 3100 BC) to the breakdown of the Ptolemaic Kingdom with the demise of Cleopatra in 30 BC.
- Egyptian apparel was loaded up with an assortment of hues.
- Decorated with valuable diamonds and gems, the styles of the old Egyptians were made for excellence as well as solace.
- Egyptian design was made to keep cool while in the hot desert.

MESOPOTAMIAN:

- Periphery enhanced the two most essential articles of clothing worn in Mesopotamia: the skirt and the shawl.
- These articles of clothing were made out of woven fleece or material, and later, for the wealthiest individuals, cotton or silk.

Old GREEK:

- Garments in Ancient Greece comprised of lengths of rectangular cloth or fleece texture.
- The Greeks wore light garments as the atmosphere was hot for the vast majority of the year.
- Their article of clothing typically comprised of two fundamental parts: a tunic (either a peplos or chiton) and a shroud (himation). ... It was made of fleece and had fastened at shoulders.

CHAPTER-1

INTRODUCTION OF WORLD TEXTILE AND COSTUME:

- The wearing of garments is solely a human trademark and is a component of most human social orders.
- Man and lady started wearing garments after the last Ice Age.
- Anthropologists accept that creature skins and vegetation were adjusted into covers as security from cold, warmth, and downpour, particularly as people moved to new atmospheres.
- Materials can be felt or spun filaments made into yarn and in this way got, circled, weave, or woven to make textures, which showed up in the Middle East during the late stone age.
- From the antiquated occasions to the current day, techniques for material creation have consistently developed, and the selections of materials accessible have affected how individuals conveyed their assets, dressed, and enriched their environmental factors.

PREHISTORIC TEXTILE:

Pre-historic textiles & costumes- Indus Valley, Egyptian, Mesopotamian, French, Greek, Roman, Japanese & Byzantine

INDUS VALLEY:

- The design of the Indus Valley individuals comprised of undergarment for men, wrap skirts and shoulder shores for ladies, shoes made of material and wood, and garments made of cotton and woolen yarn.
- Others incorporate trimmings, accessories, filets, armlets just as finger rings.

Old ROME:

- Dress in old Rome by and large contained a short-sleeved or sleeveless, knee-length tunic for men and young men, and a more drawn out, generally sleeved tunic for ladies and young ladies.
- Most urban Romans wore shoes, shoes, boots, or shoes of different kinds; in the open country, some wore obstructs.

BYZANTINE:

- The Byzantines, who would in general favor basic streaming garments to the winding and hanging of the frock, got rid of the robe inside and out.
- They picked as their generally fundamental of pieces of clothing the dalmatic, a long, streaming men's tunic, or shirt, with wide sleeves and fix, and the stola for ladies.

Old JAPAN:

- The kimono is the customary dress of Japan.
- It has long sleeves and ranges from the shoulders right down to one's heels.
- Various kinds of kimono are worn relying upon the event;
- kimonos for regular wear are significantly less complex than those for formal events.

ANTIQUATED INDIAN TEXTILES AND COSTUMES:

VEDIC PERIOD CLOTHING:

- During the Vedic time, a solitary material hung around the body, over the shoulder was stuck or secured with a belt and was viewed as agreeable clothing for the sweltering climate.
- Paridhana or vasana was a lower article of clothing which was a material hung around the abdomen with a string or belt called rasana or mekhala.

MAURYAN:

- As an upper piece of clothing, individuals' fundamental attire was uttariya, a long scarf.
- The distinction existed uniquely in the way of wearing.
- Now and again, its one end is tossed more than one shoulder and here and there it is hung over both the shoulders
- .In materials, for the most part, cotton, silk, cloth, fleece, muslin, and so forth.

Maurya Sunga Period
- Roshan Alkazi

KUSHANAS:

- The Kushan culture kept going almost 400 years.
- 5 rulers dominated. In the beginning periods, everybody wore Persian style articles of clothing, and the individuals they were administering wore Hindu style pieces of clothing from the Mauryan times.
- Step by step the two outfit styles blended and in the end when of the Guptas, the vast majority were wearing Hindu style articles of clothing.
- The regal court women and squires wore a Hindu style.

SATAVAHANAS:

- Wore straightforward long antariyas with free kayabandhs tied in a tangle at the inside alongside lovely trimmings.
- Regular citizens Their changed outfits included short
- antariyas, enormous uttariyas with expounding outskirts covering their head and back.

GUPTA:

- Garments in the Gupta time frame was for the most part cut and sewn articles of clothing.
- A long-sleeved brocaded tunic turned into the principle outfit for special individuals like the nobles and retainers.
- The principle outfit for the ruler was regularly a blue firmly woven silk antariya, maybe with a square printed design.

MUGHAL;

- Men wore long and short robes and covers including the chogha (dress), a long-sleeved coat.
- A "pagri" (turban) was worn on the head and "patka", an enhanced scarf, was worn on the abdomen.
- "Paijama" style pants were worn (leg covers that gave the English word pajama).

VICTORIAN ERA AND FRENCH REVOLUION TILL WORLD WAR 2:

- The bodices during Victorian occasions confined the developments of a lady.
- Victorian lady's design was numerous layers of dresses, skirts, pullovers, coats, wraps, slips, undergarments, gems, and embellishments worn after consistently. It was a detailed undertaking.

WORLD WAR 1:

- In WW1 Women and young ladies never wore pants and ladies wore long dresses and skirts.
- Men and young men would consistently wear coats and ties, and keep their jackets on regardless of whether it was hot outside.

WORLD WAR 2:

- Ladies during World War II regularly wore headscarves, turbans, wedged-mend shoes (versus high heels), and the kangaroo shroud.
- Security for ladies while working in the industrial facility
- was similarly as significant as style during this time.
- The kangaroo shroud was a very signature bit of wartime apparel/extra.

FRENCH REVOLUTION:

WOMENS COSTUME:

- During the long periods of the French Revolution, ladies' dress ventured into various sorts of the national outfit.
- Ladies wore varieties of white skirts, beat with progressive hued striped coats,
- just as white Greek chemise outfits, embellished with shawls, scarves, and strips.

The "pouter-pigeon" front came into style, yet indifferent regards ladies' designs were beginning to be improved by impacts from Englishwomen's nation outside wear.

The typical design toward the start of the period was a low-necked outfit.

Most outfits had skirts that opened in front to show the underskirt worn underneath.

- Front-wrapping thigh-length shortgowns or bedgowns of lightweight printed cotton texture stayed trendy at-home morning wear, worn with underskirts.

- After some time, bedgowns turned into the staple upper article of clothing of British and American female common laborers road wear.

- Ladies would likewise frequently wear a neckcloth or a progressively formal trim unobtrusiveness piece, especially on lower cut dresses, regularly for humility reasons.

MENS COSTUME:

- The conventional riding propensity comprised of a custom-fitted coat like a man's jacket, worn with a high-necked shirt, a petticoat, an underskirt, and a cap.

- On the other hand, the coat and a bogus petticoat front may be made as a solitary article of clothing,
- And later in the period a more straightforward riding coat and underskirt could be worn.

- The popular shape was a somewhat conelike middle, with huge hips. The midsection was not especially little.
- Stays were normally bound cozily, however easily; just those inspired by outrageous designs bound firmly.
- They offered back help for truly difficult work, and poor and white-collar class ladies had the option to work easily in them.
- As the casual, nation design grabbed hold in France, stays were here and there supplanted by a softly boned article of clothing called undergarment.

Free-hanging pockets were tied around the midriff and were gotten to through pocket cuts in the side-creases of the outfit or underskirt.

- The long upper likewise was disposed of, basically leaving just the toes of the foot secured.
- The shoes that were usually worn with shoes were surrendered in light of the fact that the shoes had gotten settled enough to be worn without them.
- Fans kept on being mainstream in this timeframe, nonetheless,
- They were progressively supplanted, outside at any rate, by the parasol.

- By the 1780s, expound caps supplanted the previous expand hairdos.
- Crowd tops and other "nation" styles were worn inside. Level, expansive overflowed and low-delegated straw "shepherdess" caps tied on with strips were worn with the new provincial styles.

- Men kept on wearing the coat, petticoat, and breeches.
- In any case, changes were seen in both the texture utilized just like the cut of these articles of clothing.
- More consideration was paid to singular bits of the suit, and every component experienced expressive changes.

- In the 1780s, the skirts of the coat started to be cut away in a bend from the front abdomen.
- Petticoats bit by bit abbreviated until they were midsection length and cut straight over.
- Petticoats could be made with or without sleeves. As in the past period, free, T-formed silk, cotton, or material outfit called a banyan was worn at home as a kind of robe over the shirt, petticoat, and breeches.

- Full-dress shirts had unsettled of fine texture or trim, while strip shirts finished in plain wrist groups.
- A little turnover neckline came back to mold, worn with the stock.

The wide-overflowed tricorne caps turned up on three sides were presently turned in advance and back or on the sides to shape bicornes.

- Low-obeyed calfskin shoes secured with shoe clasps were worn with silk or woolen stockings.
- Boots were worn for riding. The clasps were either cleaned metal, as a rule in silver.

KIDS COSTUME:

- Little children wore launderable dresses called gowns of cloth or cotton.
- British and American young men after maybe three started to wear rather short pantaloons and short coats,
- And for young men the skeleton suit was presented.

LOCAL TEXTILES AND COSTUMES OF INDIA:

BROCADES OF BANARAS:

- Banaras (Varanasi), a sacred city of Uttar Pradesh, is a middle for brocade and hand-made materials and saris since old occasions.
- The word brocade is gotten from the Latin word "brochus" indicating to transfix.

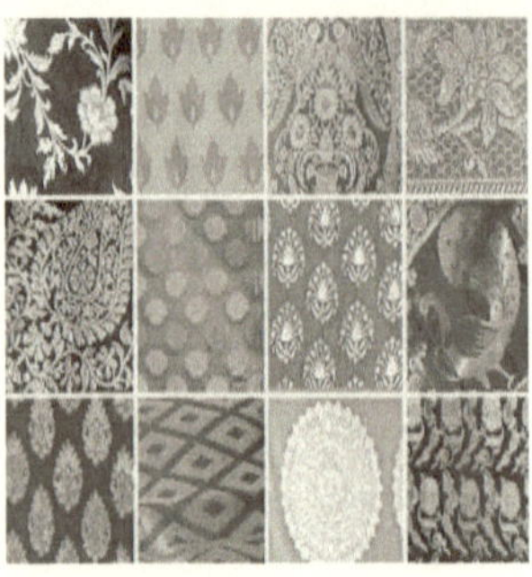

BALUCHURI:

- Baluchar Sari or Baluchuri Sari is a sort of sari, an article of clothing worn by ladies across India and Bangladesh.
- This specific sort of sari began in Bengal and is known for delineations of legendary scenes on the pallu of the sari.

CHANDERI:

- Chanderi is a customary ethnic texture described by its lightweight, sheer surface and fine rich feel.
- The texture acquired its name from the unassuming community Chanderi in Madhya Pradesh where conventional weavers practice the specialty of creating

finished sarees in cotton and silk enlivened with fine zari work.

TANCHOI:

- Tanchoi is one of the weaving procedures including a solitary or twofold twist and two to five hues on the weft which are frequently of a similar shade, on Silk texture.
- Another independent element of the Tanchoi sarees is that the texture surface foundation has a Satin finish.

KANCHIPURAM:

- The Kanchipuram silk sari is a kind of silk sari made in the Kanchipuram area in Tamil Nadu, India.
- These saris are worn as wedding and extraordinary event saris by most ladies in Tamil Nadu, Karnataka, and Andhra Pradesh.
- It has been perceived as a Geographical sign by the Government of India in 2005–2006.

HIMRU:

- Himroo is a texture made of silk and cotton, which is developed locally in Aurangabad.

- Himroo was brought to Aurangabad in the rule of Mohammad tuglaq, when he had moved his capital from Delhi to Daulatabad, Aurangabad. The word him roo started from Persian word Hum-ruh which signifies 'comparative'.

- Himroo is a replication of Kinkhwab, which was woven with unadulterated brilliant and silver strings in days of yore, and was intended for the illustrious families.

KALAMKARI:

- The specialty of Kalamkari painting is one of the most established conventional specialties of India.
- The hand-drawn pen kalamkari has developed into a market maker with non-literal square prints and screenprints in sarees, kurtas, and yardage.

www.ingramcontent.com/pod-product-compliance
Lightning Source LLC
Chambersburg PA
CBHW051144250726
48655CB00007B/3220